LINE OF DUTY

THE NATIONAL SECURITY AGENCY

CRACKING SECRET CODES

by Connie Colwell Miller

Reading Consultant
Barbara J. Fox
Reading Specialist
North Carolina State University

Content Consultant
Kenneth E. deGraffenreid
Professor of Intelligence Studies
Institute of World Politics
Washington, D.C.

Capstone press

Mankato, Minnesota

Blazers is published by Capstone Press,
151 Good Counsel Drive, P.O. Box 669, Mankato, Minnesota 56002.
www.capstonepress.com

Library of Congress Cataloging-in-Publication Data
Miller, Connie Colwell, 1976–
    The National Security Agency: cracking secret codes / by Connie
Colwell Miller.
    p. cm. — (Blazers. Line of duty)
    Summary: "Describes the NSA, including what it is and what the agency
does" — Provided by publisher.
    Includes bibliographical references and index.
    ISBN–13: 978-1-4296-1274-6 (hardcover)
    ISBN–10: 1-4296-1274-6 (hardcover)
    1. United States. National Security Agency — Juvenile literature. I. Title.
II. Series.
UB251.U5M557 2008
327.1273 — dc22   2007024746

Editorial Credits
Aaron Sautter, editor; Bobbi J. Wyss, designer; Wanda Winch, photo researcher

Photo Credits
AP Images/Evan Vucci, 14; U.S. Navy, H. Dwain Willis, HO, 5;
    The White House, Eric Draper, 16–17
Capstone Press/Karon Dubke, 24–25
Corbis/Brooks Kraft, 8, 28–29; Reuters/Jason Reed, 22–23; Richard Baker, 20;
    zefa/Gregor Schuster, 26–27
Courtesy of the National Security Agency, 6, 7, 19
Getty Images Inc./AFP/Paul J. Richards, cover, 10–11; Hulton Archive, 9;
    Time & Life Pictures/Mai/Greg Mathieson, 21
U.S. Navy Photo by Chief Photographer's Mate John E. Gay, 12–13

1 2 3 4 5 6 13 12 11 10 09 08

TABLE OF CONTENTS

BREAKING THE CODE

A U.S. soldier hears an enemy message on the radio. But the message is in **code**. The soldier can't figure out what the message means.

[**code** — a system used to send secret messages]

5

NSA headquarters in Fort Meade, Maryland

THEY SERVED IN SILENCE

Memorial honoring NSA workers

The National Security **Agency** (NSA) is asked to break the code. Workers at the NSA figure out what the message says. Their work helps stop an enemy attack.

[**agency** — a government office that provides a service]

The NSA works to find out what U.S. enemies are planning. Breaking codes tells U.S. leaders about enemy plans.

Page / Book Western Funstones OK
3   sending Banquet
7   chocks
9   got job
11   no job
13   pay good
15   "   bad
22 comeing evening of
26 1st sunday of month
28   2nd
30   3rd   5 till 6 PM
39   4th
50 sending cash
57 cannot find means
62 received your letter
67 not received letter
100 sending lenses for Telso
Detective or Mystery
4   Delivered PS note
7   am in touch with them
11 cannot get in touch
14 big plan under way
29 they won't do it
802 got his note OK

26·6·'38
Tá fear ag dul amac
as an áit seo agus
táim chun an sgríbínn
seo do tabairt dó
air é do cur ins
an puist 7 mbíí Clise.
mar deireann an
Daine seo do bfuil
sé ag dul ann ar féad
cúpla lá. Dar ndóig
ní cuirim moran.
suim air an aon ru
agus dá brig sin
níl'im d'cur mo
smaointe do feic anns
agus táim ag baine
feidir as an gaedilg
feis. b'féidir do bf
an fear seo do mar

---

3 GROVHS
25 Gloucester St
Morris Town.

GET A SMALL
ENVELOPE AND PUT
THIS NOTE INTO
IT.

macánta agus b'féidir
do rud eile é. 's
cuma liom pé rud
mar ní féidir leis an
nóta beag seo a tán
órógbéil do deanain
má d'teigeann sé
amuga. Tá fios
agat do bfuil an
pianas ann d'fear
a gabrar 7 deanain
an rud ainm d'
deanain anos. ac
sgéal eile é sin.
nuair a tangas do
áit an áit seo ar
druis ceapas gan
air mac 7fean 7
gcomporan feis ac

EXPERT CODE BREAKERS

The NSA is part of
the U.S. government.
This agency makes and
breaks secret codes.

NSA workers secretly listen to coded messages from other countries. The workers find out what the messages really say.

FACT! The NSA's military branch is called the Central Security Service (CSS).

Soldiers in the U.S. military often secretly work for the NSA.

U.S. leaders at the NSA's Threat Operations Center

NSA workers share
what they learn with U.S.
leaders. The information
helps leaders decide how
to protect the country.

The NSA is so secret that
some people joke it stands
for "No Such Agency."

 The NSA grinds used paper into pulp so U.S. secrets don't fall into the wrong hands.

The NSA also makes codes. U.S. leaders use the codes to safely share secret information. They don't want enemies to know any of their plans.

U.S. presidents and other leaders often use NSA codes to safely share secrets.

EQUIPMENT AND SKILLS

The NSA uses **supercomputers** to break the hardest codes. Computers also help workers decode e-mail messages and Internet sites.

[**supercomputer** — the fastest and most powerful computer available]

FACT! One NSA supercomputer can handle 64 billion instructions per second.

An old supercomputer once used to break codes is displayed at the NSA museum.

NSA listening station at Menwith Hill in England

The NSA uses powerful radio and **satellite** dishes. The dishes help workers learn the locations of enemy weapons and soldiers.

[**satellite** — a spacecraft used to send and receive information]

NSA satellite dish

The NSA uses **secure** telephones. These phones keep enemies from listening in on secret calls.

[**secure** — safe and well protected]

FACT! Cryptology is the name used for the science and art of making and breaking codes.

Secure telephones
at the NSA

Codes are made using letters, numbers, and symbols. NSA workers need advanced language and math skills to break codes.

FACT! The NSA is the largest employer of math experts in the United States.

KEEPING SECRETS SAFE

Main

The NSA has many ways to keep secrets safe. **Fingerprint** and eye scanners keep enemies out of U.S. computer files.

[**fingerprint** — the pattern
made by the tips of your fingers]

The NSA is always working to uncover enemy secrets.

The NSA has some of the world's smartest workers and best equipment. With the NSA on the job, no enemy secrets will stay safe for long.

FACT! About 30,000 people work for the NSA.

agency (AY-juhn-see) — a government office that provides a service to the country

code (KODE) — a system of letters, symbols, and numbers used to send secret messages

cryptology (krip-TOL-uh-jee) — the science and art of making and breaking codes

fingerprint (FING-gur-print) — the pattern made by the curved ridges on the tips of your fingers

pulp (PUHLP) — a mixture of ground up paper and water

satellite (SAT-uh-lite) — a spacecraft used to send signals and information from one place to another

secure (si-KYOOR) — safe and well protected

supercomputer (SOO-pur-kuhm-pyoo-tur) — the fastest and most powerful computer available

READ MORE

Becker, Helaine. *Secret Agent Y.O.U.: The Official Guide to Secret Codes, Disguises, Surveillance, and More.* Toronto: Maple Tree Press, 2006.

Janeczko, Paul B. *Top Secret: A Handbook of Codes, Ciphers, and Secret Writing.* Cambridge, Mass.: Candlewick Press, 2004.

INTERNET SITES

FactHound offers a safe, fun way to find Internet sites related to this book. All of the sites on FactHound have been researched by our staff.

Here's how:
1. Visit *www.facthound.com*
2. Choose your grade level.
3. Type in this book ID **1429612746** for age-appropriate sites. You may also browse subjects by clicking on letters, or by clicking on pictures and words.
4. Click on the **Fetch It** button.

FactHound will fetch the best sites for you!

INDEX